291
BRO

Hilltop Elem. Library
West Unity, OH

My First
REFERENCE LIBRARY

How People
WORSHIP

Adapted from Lynn Underwood's *Religions of the World*

JULIE BROWN
ROBERT BROWN

Gareth Stevens Children's Books
MILWAUKEE

For a free color catalog describing Gareth Stevens' list of high-quality children's books, call 1-800-341-3569 (USA) or 1-800-461-9120 (Canada).

Library of Congress Cataloging-in-Publication Data

Brown, Julie, 1962-
　　How people worship / by Julie Brown and Robert Brown. — North American ed.
　　　　p. cm.
　　　Summary: A simple introduction to religions from tribal gods and the ancient religions of Egypt, Greece, and Rome to beginnings and beliefs of such major world religions as Buddhism, Judaism, Hinduism, Islam, Confucianism, and Christianity.
　　　ISBN 0-8368-0047-8
　　　1. Religions—Juvenile literature. 2. Worship—Juvenile literature. [1. Religions.] I. Brown, Robert, 1961- . II. Title.
BL92.B76　1991
291—dc20　　　　　　　　　　　　　　　　　　　　　　　　　90-23939

North American edition first published in 1992 by
Gareth Stevens Children's Books
1555 North RiverCenter Drive, Suite 201
Milwaukee, Wisconsin 53212, USA

Text and format copyright © 1992 by Belitha Press Ltd. and Gareth Stevens, Inc. Illustrations/photographs copyright © 1992 in this format by Belitha Press Limited and Gareth Stevens, Inc. US edition copyright © 1992. First conceived, designed, and produced as *Religions of the World* by Belitha Press Limited and Gareth Stevens, Inc. First published in the United States and Canada in 1992 by Gareth Stevens, Inc. All rights reserved. No part of this book may be reproduced or used in any form or by any means without permission in writing from Gareth Stevens, Inc.

Photographic credits: The Anne Frank Foundation/Cosmospress, 35 (right); Deni Bown, 13 (left); Bridgeman Art Library, 10, 28-29, 30 (right), 40, 42, 44 (top), 45 (bottom); The British Library, 23 (right); Robert Estall, 21; ET Archive, 46-47; Chris Fairclough, 56 (bottom); Sally and Richard Greenhill, 27 (right); Michael Holford, 15 (bottom); Jimmy Holmes, 31; Mark Honan, 32 (left); Hutchinson Library, 6 (left), 7 (top and bottom right), 19 (left), 23 (left), 27 (left), 28 (left), 36, 38 (left), 50, 53; Magnum, 5 (left), 12 (right), 14, 24, 56 (top); Mansell Collection, 12 (left); Darren Marsh, 9 (top), 32 (right), 51; Mary Evans Picture Library, 13 (right), 17, 44 (bottom), 45 (top), 46 (left); Susan Mennell, 19 (right); Network Photographers, 30 (left), 38-39; Popperfoto, 43, 55, 57; Robert Harding Picture Library, 5 (right), 6 (right), 7 (left), 9 (bottom), 15 (top), 26, 33, 35 (left), 41, 47 (right), 49; Frank Spooner, 52; Wiener Library, 11, 48; ZEFA, 20, 48.

Illustrated by: Gill Tomblin
Cover illustration: Tim Waite/Third Coast © 1988
Chart on pp. 58-59: Eugene Fleury

Series editors: Neil Champion and Rita Reitci
Research editor: Scott Enk
Educational consultant: Dr. Alistair Ross
Designed by: Groom and Pickerill
Cover design: Beth Karpfinger
Picture research: Ann Usborne

Printed in the United States of America

1 2 3 4 5 6 7 8 9 97 96 95 94 93 92

Contents

1: About Religion
Learning about Religion 4
What Is Religion? 6
Forms of Belief 8
How Religions Spread 10

2: Ancient Religions
Ancient Gods 12
The Egyptians 14
Greece and Rome 16

3: Tribal Religions
Religion and Nature 18
A Way of Life 20

4: Far Eastern Religions
Buddhism 22
Buddhist Secrets 24
Confucius and Lao-tzu 26

5: Religions from India
Hinduism 28
Hindu Sects 30
India's Other Religions 32

6: Judaism
The History of the Jews 34
The Jewish Religion 36
Jewish Movements 38

7: Christianity
Christian Origins 40
The Growth of Christianity 42
The Reformers 44
Christians in the New World ... 46

8: Islam
The Prophet Muhammad 48
How Islam Has Spread 50
Islamic Sects 52

9: Religions Today
New Beliefs 54
Living Together 56
Time Chart 58

Glossary 60
Index 62

1: ABOUT RELIGION

Learning about Religion

People who do not believe in a religion often have a hard time understanding why others do. They may wonder how believers can put their faith in something that they cannot see or prove by scientific tests. Believers are amazed that anyone can live happily while not knowing about the unseen powers of our world. People learn about religions so that they can understand the beliefs of other people. You can learn about a religion without changing your own beliefs.

The Sun, the sky, the sea, and the rain are all parts of nature that can seem difficult to understand. Early peoples explained them by making them gods — beings that had special powers. ▼

The Beginnings of Religion

Early men and women could not understand nature. So they invented gods that had great powers. The Sun, wind, rain, and Moon were all thought to be gods. People gathered and gave thanks to these gods. So began the formal religions of today.

▲ Two beautiful religious texts. Left: A fourteenth-century Christian Bible. Right: An eighteenth-century Muslim Koran.

These symbols are used to identify religions and their followers. ▼

Christianity

Judaism

Hinduism

Sikhism

Buddhism

Islam

ABOUT RELIGION

What Is Religion?

▲ These Buddhists are forming a religious procession outside a temple in Myanmar (Burma).

Top, right: Muslims pray outside a mosque in Pakistan. Holy men call the Muslims to worship from the tall towers, known as minarets.

The many religions in the world are all different, but they have some things in common:

God or gods: Most religions worship some form of divinity — a holy being or beings.
Creation stories: Stories that explain how the world began.
Prayer: Most religions expect followers to pray to their God or gods, or to meditate — think deeply about spiritual things.
Places of worship: These are places where people go to worship their God or gods, to pray or meditate, or to be with other religious followers.
Priests, ministers, leaders: People with special religious duties, who may speak to the

◀ A Christian church in France. Christian places of worship can be small chapels or great churches called cathedrals.

gods or God, or who may give spiritual or moral advice.

Afterlife: This is the belief that the human spirit lives after death, either in a special place or to be reborn into another life on Earth.

Sacred writings: Stories or teachings that tell people what to believe and how to worship.

Code of life: Most religions have rules for their believers to follow in their everyday lives.

▲ Hindus worship in this finely carved temple.

◀ This Jewish religious leader is a rabbi, which means "teacher." Rabbis preach inside synagogues — Jewish places of worship.

ABOUT RELIGION

Forms of Belief

Prophetic Religions
People who follow prophetic religions believe that gods or God speaks to them through messengers called prophets. The followers pray to their gods or God for help and for advice. Judaism and Christianity are examples of prophetic religions.

Mystical Religions
Followers of mystical religions do not believe in gods or holy messengers. Instead, they follow a special way of life. In mystical religions, wise men or women help their followers

A Hindu *sadhu*, or holy man, sits meditating. He has some prayer beads and a conch shell, both sacred to the Hindu god Vishnu. ▶

develop spiritual wisdom. One mystical religion is Buddhism. Most religions of today combine prophetic and mystical traits.

This Christian ceremony recalls the suffering and death of Jesus Christ. Christians believe Christ's birth and death were foretold by prophets.

◀ Shinto women priests from Japan. The Shinto religion is both mystical and prophetic.

ABOUT RELIGION

How Religions Spread

▲ St. Augustine, who was sent by the pope from Rome to Britain in the sixth century AD. He converted the English people to Christianity.

Some religions that started out very small have spread all over the world. This has happened for several reasons.

Travel and Conquest
Some religions spread because people traveled from one place to another. They took their religions with them. Also, when one group conquered another, the conquerors often forced the people they conquered to accept their religion.

Conversion and Searching
Some religions have spread because their followers work to

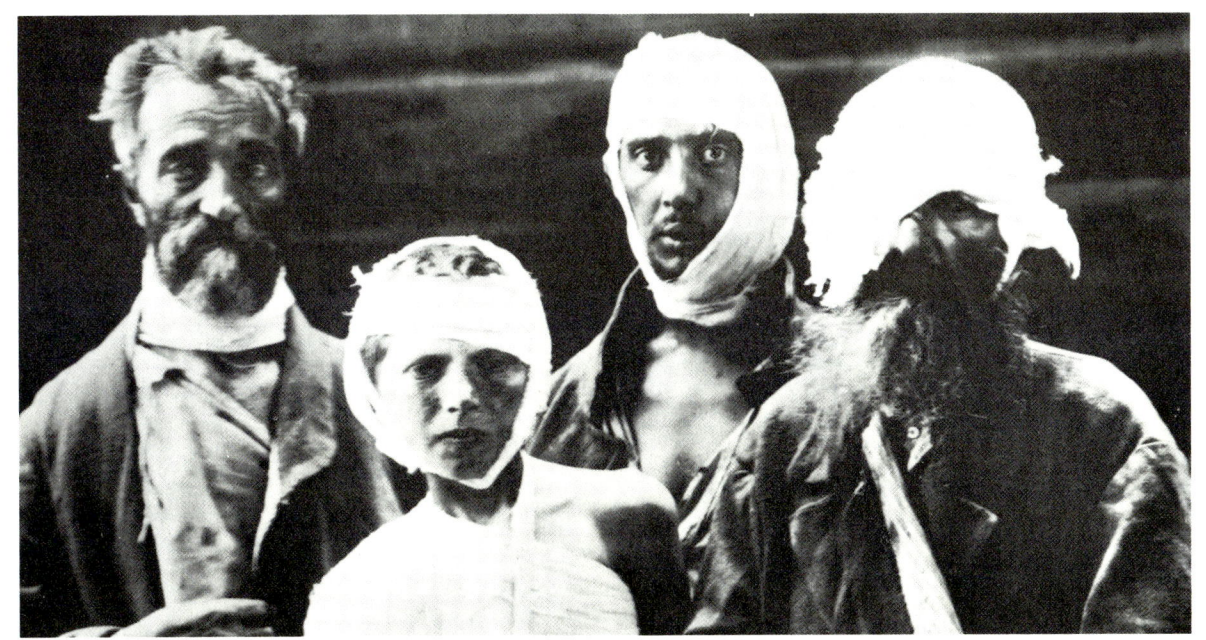

▲ These Ukrainian Jews were beaten by Polish troops in 1919 because of their religious beliefs.

convert people to their religion. We call this proselytism. Other religions have grown because people have searched for new ideas to improve their lives.

Missionaries

Missionaries travel all over the world to try to convert people to their religion. They also try to improve the lives of others. One medical missionary in Africa, David Livingstone (1813-73), later became an explorer famous for his discoveries.

◀ People listening to a mystical spiritual leader. Mystical religions are spreading because many people are searching for new spiritual ideas.

11

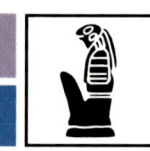

2: ANCIENT RELIGIONS

Ancient Gods

Early religions were based on what was important to people. Farmers used to worship the gods of Sun and rain. Warriors worshiped war gods. Many of these early religions died out.

Sir James Frazer (1854-1941) spent much of his life studying and writing about ancient religions. ▼

Modern druids carrying out a rite at Stonehenge, England. Druids were Celtic priests. In the first century AD, they were stamped out by the Romans. Today, some people are reviving old druid customs. ▶

The Norse Gods

Less than 2,000 years ago, many people in Europe worshiped Norse gods. Thor, the chief god, ruled winds and storms. Some of our weekdays are named after Norse gods. Wednesday is named after the Norse god Woden, Thursday after the god Thor, and Friday after the goddess Freya, Thor's wife.

Ancient American Gods

In the sixteenth century, the civilizations of the Maya, Aztecs, and Inca were destroyed by Spaniards. Their religions, which included Sun and nature worship, vanished with them. Only their great shrines and temples remain.

This picture of Maya gods and nobles is from the 1400s. Pictures like this, statues, and other artwork are all that is left of the Maya religion.

◀ Mistletoe, once used in ancient religions of northern Europe, is now part of celebrating Christmas.

Did You Know?

The word "Yuletide," now referring to Christmas, comes from the ancient Norse celebration of the winter solstice, the shortest day of the year.

ANCIENT RELIGIONS

The Egyptians

Ancient Egypt was an advanced civilization. The Egyptians left a large number of remains. Many of their writings and pictures are about their religion.

Osiris and Life after Death
Ancient Egyptians worshiped a great many gods. Their most powerful god was Osiris, god of the Nile River and king of the dead. Egyptians firmly believed in life after death. Their priests embalmed bodies with salt and spices and then wrapped them in cloth. We call these bodies mummies. The important dead were then placed in huge tombs. Their valuable belongings and some food were buried with them. Egyptians believed that the dead would need these things in the next world.

Ancient Egypt prospered on the banks of the Nile River. This photo shows the Nile as it has been for thousands of years. ▼

14

▲ The god Osiris, king of the dead, sits on his throne. Horus, the falcon-headed god of sky, light, and goodness, approaches. This painting is from the Book of the Dead, dating from around 1250 BC.

◀ The mummy and case of an Egyptian priestess from about 1050 BC.

The Sumerians

The ancient Sumerians lived in the Middle East. They worshiped many gods and believed in life after death. Sumerians believed that in the afterlife, the dead sat in darkness, eating dirt.

ANCIENT RELIGIONS

Greece and Rome

The ancient Greeks and Romans believed in many gods, each with control over some natural force. Poets of the time wrote about the lives and deeds of these gods. These tales are now called myths.

Greece

Zeus and his wife Hera headed the Greek family of gods. The Greeks believed their gods lived on Mount Olympus in northern Greece. They built beautiful temples for them. The Greeks also believed that the dead went to a place called Hades. They reached Hades by being rowed

The ancient Greek and Roman gods differed mostly in name. Here, the Greek name is given first, followed by the Roman one. From left: Poseidon/Neptune, god of the sea; Hera/Juno, wife of Zeus/Jupiter, father of the gods; Artemis/Diana, goddess of hunting; Aphrodite/Venus, goddess of love; Hermes/Mercury, the wing-heeled messenger; and Athena/Minerva, the goddess of war and artisans.

Poseidon/Neptune

Hera/Juno   Zeus/Jupiter

across the River Styx by the boatman Charon. People put coins on the eyes of the dead to pay Charon for his rowing.

The Romans

The Roman gods were very much like the Greek gods. One difference was that about 2,000 years ago the Romans decided to make their emperors into gods. This gave the emperors more power over their people.

▲ Augustus ruled the Roman Empire from 27 BC to AD 14. He was the first emperor to be called a god by his people.

Aphrodite/Venus

Hermes/Mercury

Athena/Minerva

Artemis/Diana

3: TRIBAL RELIGIONS

Religion and Nature

Some tribes that exist today have changed very little over thousands of years. They have been able to keep their religious beliefs because they live far from settlers or other outsiders.

Ties with Nature

The lives of these people depend on nature. Many hunt wild animals and eat wild plants, and

The San, nomadic people who wander the Kalahari Desert in Africa. Their religion survives through story telling. ▼

◀ A religious ceremonial dance by members of the Kayapo tribe near the Amazon River in Brazil.

▲ These stone statues are on Easter Island in the South Pacific. Some people think that they may be religious symbols.

some grow crops. Their religion is based on the natural world. They believe that everything in nature — including each plant and animal — is controlled by a god or spirit. Their religions show them how to live in peace with these gods or spirits. Some tribes use magic to try to control nature. Tribal spirit healers use religion to cure sickness. In recent years, the changes brought by explorers, missionaries, and settlers have upset these tribal traditions. It is difficult for these people to keep their beliefs and customs, but some still do.

▲ This doll from Zaire, Africa, is used to bring good luck.

TRIBAL RELIGIONS

A Way of Life

North American Indians

There are many different Native American religions. But nearly all of them believe in an almighty power. This is a spirit force that is the source of all life. This almighty force can show itself in many forms. Its light and power are symbolized by the Sun. Its strength is represented by the Earth. Its wisdom is shown by certain kinds of animals. People contact this spirit force by praying or meditating, or by going without food until they receive a

▲ Totem poles in Canada carved with images of spirit ancestors by Northwest Coast Indian artists.

An Inuit mask worn in religious ceremonies. The face in the center stands for the soul of the Inuit spiritual leader. ▶

◀ Images of Dreamtime ancestors created by Australian Aboriginals. Decorations like these are considered sacred.

This rock carving is from a large group of images in Peterborough, Ontario. They are from 600 to 1,100 years old, and they show traditional Native American spiritual beliefs. ▼

vision. A spirit healer carries out rituals for curing. Many tribes hold religious dances and feasts. Souls of the good dead go to a happy place. But the souls of evil persons stay near their homes and can cause trouble.

Aboriginals from Australia

Aboriginals believe they are part of the land. They believe that rocks, trees, and water have messages that explain the meaning of life. Each person has an ancestor from the Dreamtime. This is the time during which the world was created. Aboriginals have ceremonies that help them communicate with the natural world around them.

4: FAR EASTERN RELIGIONS

Buddhism

The Four Noble Truths
1. All things suffer.
2. Suffering and rebirth are caused by desire.
3. End suffering by ending desire.
4. To end desire, follow the Noble Eightfold Path.

Prince Siddhartha Gautama founded Buddhism in the sixth century BC. As a Hindu, the rich young prince believed in rebirth. He saw how people suffered from sickness and old age. He knew they would be reborn to suffer many times. So he left his home and family to find a way to end suffering. He found that the best way to live was the middle way — without riches or poverty. After many years of meditation, he discovered the

Young Buddhist monks with begging bowls. These monks may eat only food they can get by begging. ▼

◀ A statue of Buddha in Thailand. There are at least 20,000 Buddhist temples in that country.

> **Three Baskets**
> The Buddhist holy books are the Tripitaka, or "three baskets." They were first written on palm leaves and kept in baskets. They contain Buddha's teachings, rules for monks, and comments.

Four Noble Truths. He taught these to people and became known as the Buddha, or "the Enlightened One." He traveled over the country, telling people how to end their suffering by following the Noble Eightfold Path of right beliefs, right aims, right speech, right conduct, right concentration, right effort, right thinking, and right work. The Buddha said that people should seek righteousness and wisdom through meditation.

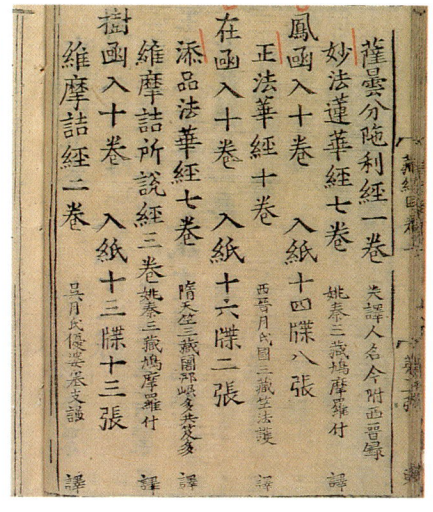

▲ A page from the Tripitaka. This copy is Korean and dates from the eleventh century AD.

23

FAR EASTERN RELIGIONS

Buddhist Sects

As Buddhism spread throughout the Far East, people practiced the religion in different ways. There are two main groups in Buddhism. Theravada, or Southern, Buddhism follows only the teachings of Buddha. This is practiced in Myanmar, Thailand, Sri Lanka, and India. Mahayana, or Northern, Buddhism includes teachings of later Buddhists. It is followed mainly in Tibet, China, Japan, and Korea. Each group contains many different sects.

A monk tends a Zen Buddhist meditation garden. The patterns in the stones help clear the mind.

Shinto

Shinto is the national religion of Japan. It combines Buddhism with an old religion that worships Amaterasu, the Sun goddess, and the spirits of living things.

◀ Many Buddhists have shrines in their homes. This girl is praying and making an offering of flowers.

These are Yellow Hat Buddhists from Tibet. They belong to a sect interested mainly in personal salvation. ▼

Buddhism in Japan

In Japan, there are at least six different sects: Tendai, Shingon, Jodo, Jodo Shinshu, Zen, and Nichiren. All follow the same basic teachings, but they have different practices. For example, Zen Buddhists concentrate on meditation for enlightenment, but Shingon Buddhists focus on symbols and ritual.

FAR EASTERN RELIGIONS

Confucius and Lao-tzu

When the Buddha was teaching in India, Lao-tzu and Confucius were teaching in China.

Confucius

K'ung Fu-tzu, or Confucius, was born in 551 BC. When he was only 22 years old, he founded a school of philosophy. Confucians believe in *jen*, meaning courtesy and loyalty at all times. They also believe in *hsaio*, which tells Confucians how to respect their elders and superiors. Confucius' teachings were written down in books called the Analects.

A Confucian temple in China. Confucians come here to make offerings of food and gifts to their ancestors. This makes their ancestors happy in the afterlife.

This painting shows Confucius teaching, with his followers around him.

26

▲ Decorations on a Taoist temple in China.

◀ This is a Taoist spirit medium from Singapore. He is in a trance, trying to contact spirits for his followers.

Lao-tzu

Taoism was founded by Lao-tzu. He believed that people should practice *wu wei*, or nonaction, and accept life as it is. This leads to harmony with the universe, and will in time bring about changes for the better. The Taoist books are the Tao Te Ching and the Chuang Tzu.

5: RELIGIONS FROM INDIA

Hinduism

Over 3,000 years ago, tribes of people called Aryans invaded India from central Asia. They brought their religion with them. Their religion centered around telling stories, chanting hymns, and reciting poems. In time, these were written down and are still studied. Hinduism today is a mixture of the Aryan religion and other local religions that were practiced long ago.

▲ This Hindu priest, called a Brahman, is wading in the Ganges River, which is regarded as sacred.

This richly colored picture is from the Hindu scripture that tells of the deeds of the prince Rama. ▶

There are many kinds of Hinduism, but all Hindus believe in Brahman, the great universal force. Many also believe in some lesser gods and spirits. Most of today's 650 million Hindus live in India. Many believe in the caste system. This means they believe people are born into certain levels of society, and they must remain there. But when people die, their souls will enter new life forms. This rebirth is called reincarnation. You might come back as a rich person or an animal, depending on your deeds, or *karma*, in your last life.

▲ This Hindu man pierces his skin with silver skewers because he believes that the pain will purify his soul. This is called mortification of the flesh.

Gandhi and Caste

Mahatma Gandhi was willing to change the caste system by working with members of the lowest caste, called the Untouchables. Most Hindus thought the Untouchables were outcasts, but Gandhi called them "Children of God." Gandhi also helped free India from British rule. ▼

RELIGIONS FROM INDIA

Hindu Sects

◀ This painting shows the Hindu god Vishnu in the form of the wise man Krishna. He is wooing a maiden with his music.

▲ Here is a carving of Ganesh, the Hindu god of wisdom. He is also a symbol of luck and riches.

Vishnu

One sect of Hindus worships the god Vishnu. He is the preserver of life. Vishnu appears in ten different forms, including the fish, the tortoise, the dwarf, the prince Rama, and the wise man Krishna. Vishnu's wife is the goddess of prosperity.

Shiva

Another Hindu sect worships the god Shiva, the destroyer. Some artwork shows Shiva as a frightening figure surrounded by evil demons. At other times, he is shown as calm and loving.

The Mother Goddess

A third sect of Hindus worships the mother goddess Shakti. Sometimes she appears as a beautiful maiden, and other times she appears as an evil old woman named Kali or Durga, standing on a demon. Each fall, she is honored by the Dashara festival, which lasts ten days.

▲ This street shrine in Nepal is loaded with food offerings during Diwali, the Hindu festival that celebrates the goddess Lakshmi, Vishnu's wife.

Home Worship

Most Hindu homes have a family shrine, often just a decorated corner of a room. At the shrine, an image of a god is anointed with oil, while family members chant hymns. Then people meditate while incense burns. Flowers or food is offered to the god.

◀ These women are making decorations for their homes for Diwali, the Festival of Lights. This celebration includes the Hindu New Year.

RELIGIONS FROM INDIA

India's Other Religions

The Sikhs

The Sikh religion was founded 500 years ago by Nanak. Sikhs believe in one God and in reincarnation. Sikhs do not drink or smoke. They do not have priests or idols, and they do not follow the Hindu caste system. Sikh men carry knives or swords because they think of themselves as warriors. Sikh children have a coming-of-age ceremony. All boys take the name Singh — "lion." And all girls take the name Kaur — "princess."

▲ A Hindu cremation ceremony in Indonesia. The dead are burned on wicker platforms. Hinduism has spread far beyond its home in India.

In England, a group of Sikhs holds a religious ceremony. Sikh men do not shave their beards. ▶

◀ This young Jain wears a mask so he won't harm insects by accidentally swallowing them. Jains will not eat meat because they believe that all living creatures have souls.

A *dakhma*, or tower of silence, where the Parsees leave their dead for the vultures. Parsees believe that burial spoils the earth. ▼

The Jains and the Parsees

Jainism began 2,500 years ago. Jains believe in reincarnation. They don't have any gods, but they think all living things have souls and should not be harmed.

The Parsee religion comes from an ancient religion of Persia, now Iran. Parsees believe in one God, Ahura Mazda. They believe that people who live a good life go to paradise after death, but evil persons go to hell. Parsees place their dead in towers for vultures to eat.

6: JUDAISM

The History of the Jews

Nearly 4,000 years ago, a man named Abraham worshiped the one God, called Yahweh. They had a covenant, or agreement, that if Abraham and all his descendants worshiped only Yahweh, they would be God's chosen people and could have the land of Canaan to live in.

The Exodus

The Jews worshiped Yahweh for many years. Then a terrible famine came to their region and

Passover
During their eight-day celebration of Passover, Jewish people remember their release from the Egyptians. There is a special meal called the seder. During this, the youngest son asks, "Why is this night different from all other nights?"

The father replies, "Because we were slaves in Egypt and God brought us forth out of Egypt."

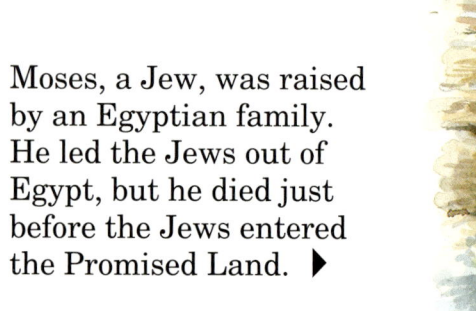

Moses, a Jew, was raised by an Egyptian family. He led the Jews out of Egypt, but he died just before the Jews entered the Promised Land. ▶

34

◀ Jewish pilgrims in Israel pray at the Western Wall, also called the Wailing Wall.

The Spread of Judaism

Jews settling in other countries were often persecuted, so they moved on. Today there are 5.7 million Jews in the United States, 3.3 million in Israel, 3 million in Europe (including 1.7 million in the USSR), and the rest throughout Africa, Asia, and South America.

forced them to move to Egypt in search of food. The Egyptians turned the Jews into slaves. Later, Moses, a great prophet, led the Jews out of Egypt and back to the Promised Land of Canaan. On the way, God gave the Ten Commandments to Moses. This journey is called the Exodus. Centuries later, the Romans drove the Jews away from their land, and they lived in other countries. In 1948, the Jews established the country of Israel as their homeland in the area of ancient Canaan.

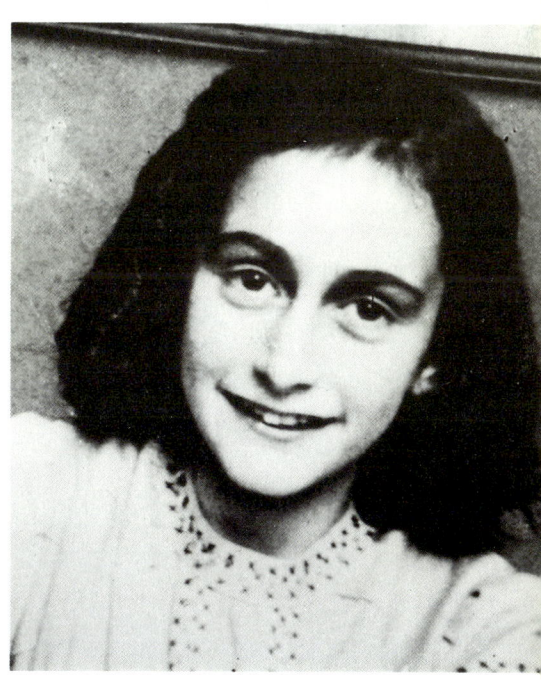

▲ Anne Frank, a Jewish girl, hid in an attic with her family in Europe during World War II. She wrote about how the Jews were persecuted.

JUDAISM

The Jewish Religion

Worship in an Orthodox ▶ synagogue. Men and women sit apart and cover their heads to show respect.

The Creation
The Jewish creation story is also part of the Christian and Islamic religions. It says that God created the world in six days. Adam and Eve, the first people, lived in the Garden of Eden until an evil serpent led them into sin.

Scriptures and Scholars
The Jewish religion is based on scriptures called the Tanakh. There are three parts: the Torah, listing the Ten Commandments and other laws for everyday life;

Bar Mitzvah
At age 13, Jewish boys have a bar mitzvah, a coming-of-age ceremony, so they can act as adults in religious events. ▶

36

prophetic books; and other writings. Jewish scholars study these scriptures constantly and give new interpretations of them. This has led to different forms of Judaism.

Worship

A Jewish leader is called a *rabbi*, meaning "teacher." Rabbis lead the services and give their people spiritual and practical advice. Jews worship in buildings called synagogues. Every synagogue has the Torah written on a set of scrolls. Jews worship during a day called the Sabbath. This day starts at sunset Friday and lasts until sunset Saturday.

Kosher Food

Jewish law has many rules about food. Pork and shellfish cannot be eaten — the animals are unclean because they are scavengers. Other animals must be slaughtered by special butchers who drain off the blood. Food prepared according to the dietary laws is called *kosher*.

Three symbols of the Jewish faith: a candlestick with seven branches (*menorah*), and the skullcap (*yarmulke*) and prayer shawl (*tallith*) worn by Jewish men.

JUDAISM

Jewish Movements

> **Ethiopian Jews**
> There are many black Jews in Ethiopia, Africa. They say they descend from followers of the queen of Sheba, who converted to Judaism when visiting the court of King Solomon in Canaan.

A Conservative Jewish couple celebrates Rosh Hashanah, the Jewish New Year, with special food and prayers.

Modern Judaism has several movements. Orthodox Jews strictly follow all the scriptures' laws. The Reform movement, started in eighteenth-century Europe, has a more relaxed outlook toward Jewish laws. Reform Jewish women may do more in the religion and even

become rabbis. Conservative Judaism started in the United States in the 1800s. These Jews take a middle path. And some groups feel that mysticism will bring them closer to God. Hasidic Jews, based in eastern Europe, spend a lot of time in devout prayer and meditation.

▲ Hasidic Jews, a group within Orthodox Judaism. They like to gather in small groups to worship God through intense joy and praise. Hasidic Judaism began in eastern Europe and has followers throughout the world, including North America.

7: CHRISTIANITY

Christian Origins

The Jewish scriptures predict a Messiah to come from the town of Bethlehem. He would be their leader, who would restore the kingdom of Solomon. When Jesus Christ was born there about 2,000 years ago, many thought he was that Messiah.

Jesus, sitting in the center, is surrounded by his 12 closest followers. They are eating the Last Supper before Jesus was crucified. One of these men, Judas, betrayed Jesus to his enemies.

> **A New Commandment**
>
> Jesus declared a new religious law: to love God with all your heart, soul, and strength, and to love your neighbor as yourself.

◀ The Sea of Galilee, in present-day Israel. Jesus preached and performed miracles here.

> **The Trinity**
>
> Christians believe that God has three persons: the Father; Jesus, the Son; and the Holy Spirit.

A Religion of Love

Jesus practiced the Jewish faith. But he also taught that a moral life was more important than rigid religious rules. He taught forgiveness of enemies and love for God and one's fellow humans. He healed the sick and did other miracles. As his followers increased, the rulers of Israel and Palestine condemned Jesus, who was accused of trying to start a rebellion. The Romans nailed Jesus to a cross, where he died.

▲ Three symbols of Christianity: the fish, the cross, and the *chi-rho* — Greek letters that stand for Christ.

Christianity Spreads

The followers of Jesus say he rose from the dead and later went up to heaven. His followers then spread his teachings to other people throughout the world.

CHRISTIANITY

The Growth of Christianity

Some Christians live in religious groups called orders. Men are monks and live in monasteries. Women are nuns and live in convents. ▶

▲ This sacred picture of Mary, the mother of Jesus, is called an icon. It was painted in Russia in the nineteenth century.

When the first Christians began spreading their new religion to others, they were persecuted and sometimes put to death. In AD 313, Constantine, the Roman emperor, became a Christian. Later, Christianity became the official religion of the empire. Church leaders made their headquarters in Rome. In time, the bishop of Rome, called the pope, became accepted as the head of the church. During the Middle Ages, some Christians formed groups called orders.

The Bible
The Christian scriptures were gathered into a book called the Bible around AD 400. A part called the Old Testament contains Jewish scriptures. A part called the New Testament includes the four Gospels, telling about the life and teachings of Jesus Christ; accounts of his followers' activities after he left this life; letters to Christian churches; and a book called Revelation, which contains prophecies for the future.

They became monks and nuns, devoting their lives to their faith.

East and West
In 1054, the church split into two groups. The Eastern group wanted to stay closer to the traditional ways. It called itself the Eastern Orthodox church. The Western group felt that a few changes needed to be made in the religion. It called itself the Roman Catholic church. Both churches still practice their own styles of Christianity today.

The pope, head of the Roman Catholic church. He lives in Vatican City. ▼

CHRISTIANITY

The Reformers

▲ Christian reformers. Above: Martin Luther. Below: John Calvin. ▼

In the sixteenth century, the Christian church divided again. A new group formed, called the Protestants. They believed the Catholic church was greedy for money and power.

For many years, the Protestants and the Catholics fought wars over their differences. During this time, many people were tortured and killed for their beliefs. In Spain, the Catholic church formed a special court called the Inquisition. If it found a person guilty of heresy, or unbelief, that person would be burned alive. In England, many Catholics were executed. This period is known as the Reformation, because many people were trying to reform Christianity.

Protestant Leaders
During and after the Reformation, several new Christian churches formed. In 1517, a German monk named Martin Luther criticized Catholic leaders. He thought people were saved from sin and would go to

heaven by having faith in God, not by giving money to the church. The people who followed his ideas were called Lutherans.

A French scholar named John Calvin developed his own ideas in 1536. He believed that some people were fated to be saved from sin before they were born.

The pope would not let England's King Henry VIII divorce his wife. So the king formed a new church, called the Church of England. He also took over the wealth of the Catholic church in England.

▲ Thomas Cranmer helped King Henry VIII form the Church of England in the early 1500s.

In the seventeenth century, Spanish Catholics set up the Inquisition. Nonbelievers were called heretics and burned at the stake. ▼

CHRISTIANITY

Christians in the New World

A group of Puritans prepares to board the *Mayflower* to sail to the New World. ▶

▲ John Wesley (1703-91) set up a new Protestant group known as the Methodist church.

When early settlers came to the New World, they brought their religions along with them. One famous group was the Puritans, who set out to "purify" the Christian faith. In the 1600s, they came to North America to escape persecution in England. Freedom of religion has been valued in the United States ever since. Today, North America has many different religions.

Living Simply

The Amish, Mennonites, and Hutterites are groups of Protestants who believe in simple living. They formed in Europe during the 1500s, but the groups now live mostly in the United States and Canada. They avoid modern technology and don't care about wealth. They all work together for the good of their communities.

Fundamentals

Some groups focus on Christian basics, or fundamentals. In the late 1700s, John Wesley started the Methodists. At about the same time, Ann Lee brought the Shakers to New York. Today, some preachers have built huge followings by preaching personal acceptance of Jesus Christ to large groups. One example is Billy Graham, known worldwide.

▲ An Amish couple in their horse-drawn buggy. Their simple life is part of their religion.

8: ISLAM

The Prophet Muhammad

Followers say that the Prophet Muhammad proclaimed the Islamic faith. Muhammad was born in the city of Mecca around AD 570. He grew disgusted with the Arab worship of many gods and spirits. After meditating for years, he received a message from Allah, the one true God. Allah told Muhammad to preach to others about returning to the

The Great Mosque in Mecca, Saudi Arabia, where thousands of pilgrims gather every year to worship Allah. Mecca is the holiest city in Islam. ▼

◀ Muslims pray facing Mecca. Five times a day, they are called to prayer by a crier, called a *muezzin*.

▼ Children learn the Koran.

The Koran

The Koran has 114 *suras*, or chapters. The Koran tells Muslims how to worship and how to do their duty to other people.

Ramadan

During the Islamic month of Ramadan, Muslims may not eat during the daytime. Muhammad thought this created self-discipline. At its end, Muslims celebrate Allah's message to Muhammad.

one true God. Muhammad then repeated Allah's words to his friend Abu Bakr, who wrote everything down in a book that is called the Koran. This is the holy book for Muslims, those who follow Islam.

ISLAM

How Islam Has Spread

When Muhammad began to preach, the people of Mecca forced him to flee to the city of Medina. This flight is called the Hegira, and it marks the start of today's Muslim calendar. Muhammad believed it was his duty to spread Islam by going to war. Such a holy war is called a *jihad*. He conquered Mecca first. After Muhammad died, Mecca was ruled by a series of caliphs, who continued to spread their religion by war.

These tiles, decorated with Arabic writing, come from a mosque in Iran. A mosque is an Islamic place of worship.

The Muslims spread their religion throughout the Mediterranean. This building in Spain features Muslim architecture.

50

The Islamic Empire

After many years, the empire of Islam had spread to Africa, India, Spain, Mongolia, and China. Christian crusaders from Europe fought against the Muslims for 200 years. They captured some Muslim land and the city of Jerusalem. But the Muslims won it all back. In the fifteenth century, the Spaniards drove the Muslims out of Spain. In time, the Islamic empire broke up. But many people still kept the religion. Today, Islam has about a billion followers. Most live outside the Near East.

▲ Every year, Spanish actors re-create the time when the Muslims were driven out of Spain in the 1400s. The Muslims were also called Moors.

Jinns

The Koran talks about jinns, or genies. These are spirits created out of fire to serve Allah. Many folk tales from Islam are stories about genies who grant wishes and work magic. Wicked jinns are called demons, and they often tempt people.

ISLAM

Islamic Sects

An ayatollah, or leader, of the Shi'ite Muslims. Ayatollahs are powerful because they can make laws based on their understanding of the Koran. About 20% of all Muslims are Shi'ites. Most of the other 80% are Sunnites. ▶

Islam's Five Pillars

Shahada: Declaring one's belief that there is no God but Allah and that Muhammad is his Prophet.
Salat: Muslims pray five times a day, while facing the city of Mecca.
Sawm: During Ramadan, Muslims do not eat or drink in the daytime.
Zakat: Muslims give part of their money to charity.
Hajj: Muslims must make a journey to Mecca, if they can.

Sunnites
Sunnites accept the Koran, the Islamic teachings, and the Five Pillars, or basic rules, of Islam. They believe that all caliphs after Muhammad were simply elected leaders.

Shi'ites
The Shi'ites believe that Ali, Muhammad's nephew, was the next true leader, and that Ali's descendants possess secret

▲ Many Islamic women wear the *chador*, a piece of cloth that covers them from head to toe. You can see only their eyes.

knowledge and are special holy men. Shi'ites follow a strict reading of the Koran.

Ahmadis

Mirza Ghulam Ahmad, who lived in India, started another Islamic sect in the late 1800s. He wanted to unite all religions under Islam. He did not believe in a holy war, but in the power of writing. His followers are in Africa and the West.

9: RELIGIONS TODAY

New Beliefs

Throughout history, people have developed new religions and sects. Some, like Islam, have lasted a long time, but others have disappeared quickly. This process is still happening today.

New Sects

Sects develop when some followers want to make changes in a religion. For example, they may say certain activities, such as

Bottom right: Hare Krishna followers in the West. They wear Eastern dress and the men shave their heads. ▼

A family of Rastafarians. They believe that God is in all people and that black people are especially favored. ▼

drinking alcohol, should not be allowed.

New Religions
In the 1800s, the Baha'i faith started in what is now Iran. It says that all the world's great

◀ A mass wedding for Unification church members and their absent partners. Korean Sun Myung Moon started this church.

religious leaders were sent by one God to teach the people. The Hare Krishna movement in the West is based on Hindu traditions. Its followers chant in the streets. The Rastafarian religion began in the Caribbean. It is based on ideas from the Bible, but says that an emperor of Ethiopia, named Ras Tafari, was the Messiah.

Cults
Cults are often led by a strong leader, who has specific and sometimes strange ideas about religion. Many cults attract people who are searching for a new way of living. Some cults are harmless, but others can cause problems for members and their families. Some cult leaders want their members to stop being with their families so they can spend all their time working for the cult. Sadly, some cults exist only to make the cult leader rich.

RELIGIONS TODAY

Living Together

Mahatma Gandhi was a spiritual and religious leader of India. He tried to get his country's Hindus and Muslims to live together peacefully. ▶

Multiculturalism
Countries with people from many nations are called multicultural. The leaders can try to make people fit in with the country's culture. Or they can let them keep their own culture, including the right to follow their own religion.

Respecting Other Beliefs
Some people, religions, and countries respect all types of beliefs. But others do not. Some people with a rigid set of beliefs will shut themselves off

This Christian church is ▶ located in northern India. This area is mostly Hindu.

56

◀ Bob Geldof, a rock musician, raised millions of dollars for hungry people in Africa. This shows how charity can bridge all faiths.

Mother Teresa has spent her life helping the poor and sick people of India. ▼

from the rest of society. Others try to force those around them to think and act in their way. Religious hatred has long brought about many wars and much social unrest around the world. In many countries, there are people who believe in different religions. People with different beliefs must live together. Learning about other religions helps them do this.

Agnosticism

An agnostic is not sure if there is divinity or not. Many would like to believe but say it cannot be proved. The Catholic church says there are about 819 million agnostics in the world.

Time Chart

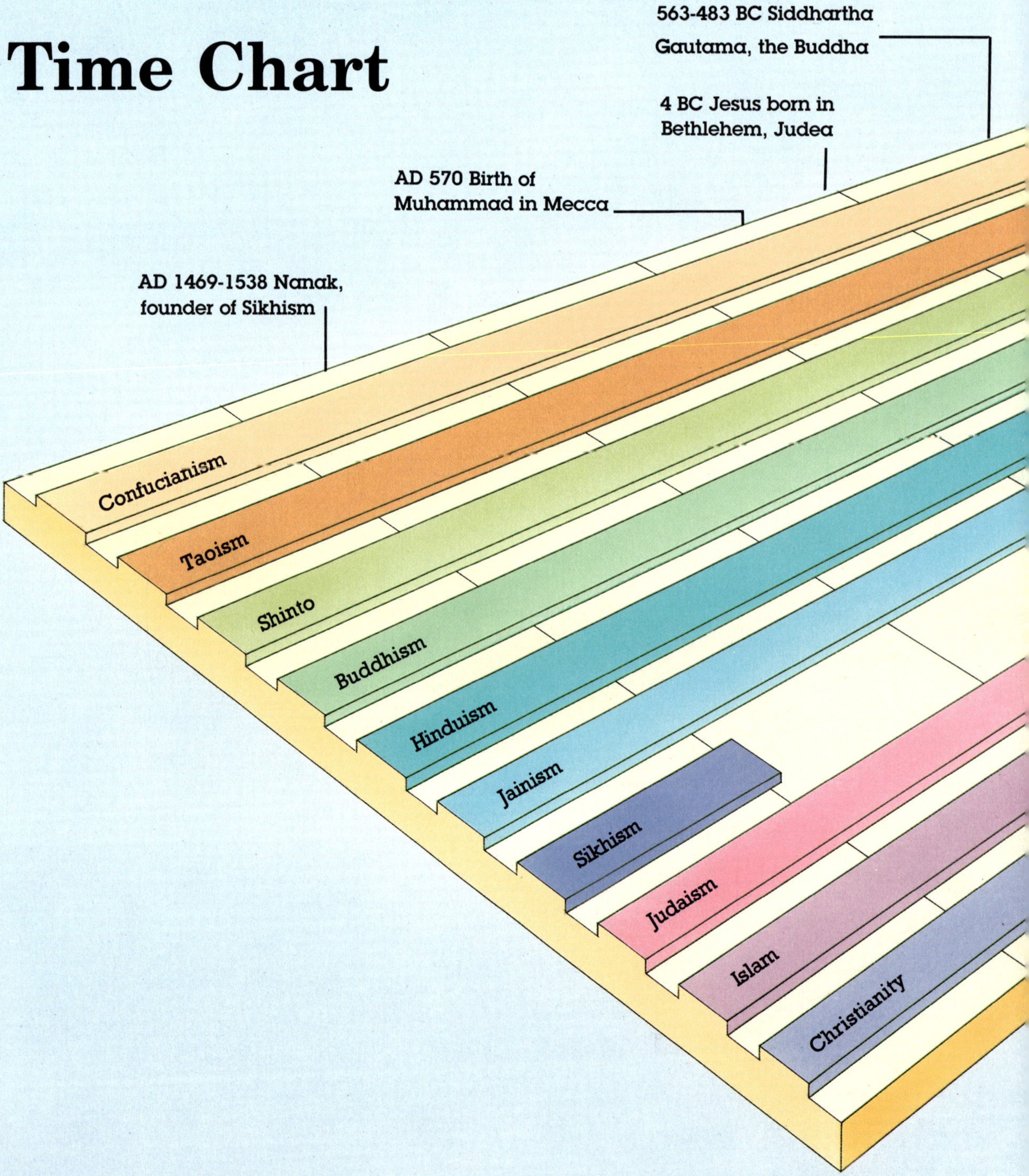

563-483 BC Siddhartha Gautama, the Buddha

4 BC Jesus born in Bethlehem, Judea

AD 570 Birth of Muhammad in Mecca

AD 1469-1538 Nanak, founder of Sikhism

- Confucianism
- Taoism
- Shinto
- Buddhism
- Hinduism
- Jainism
- Sikhism
- Judaism
- Islam
- Christianity

This chart shows the starting dates for most of the major religions of the world. Key events, like the birth of leaders, are marked out.

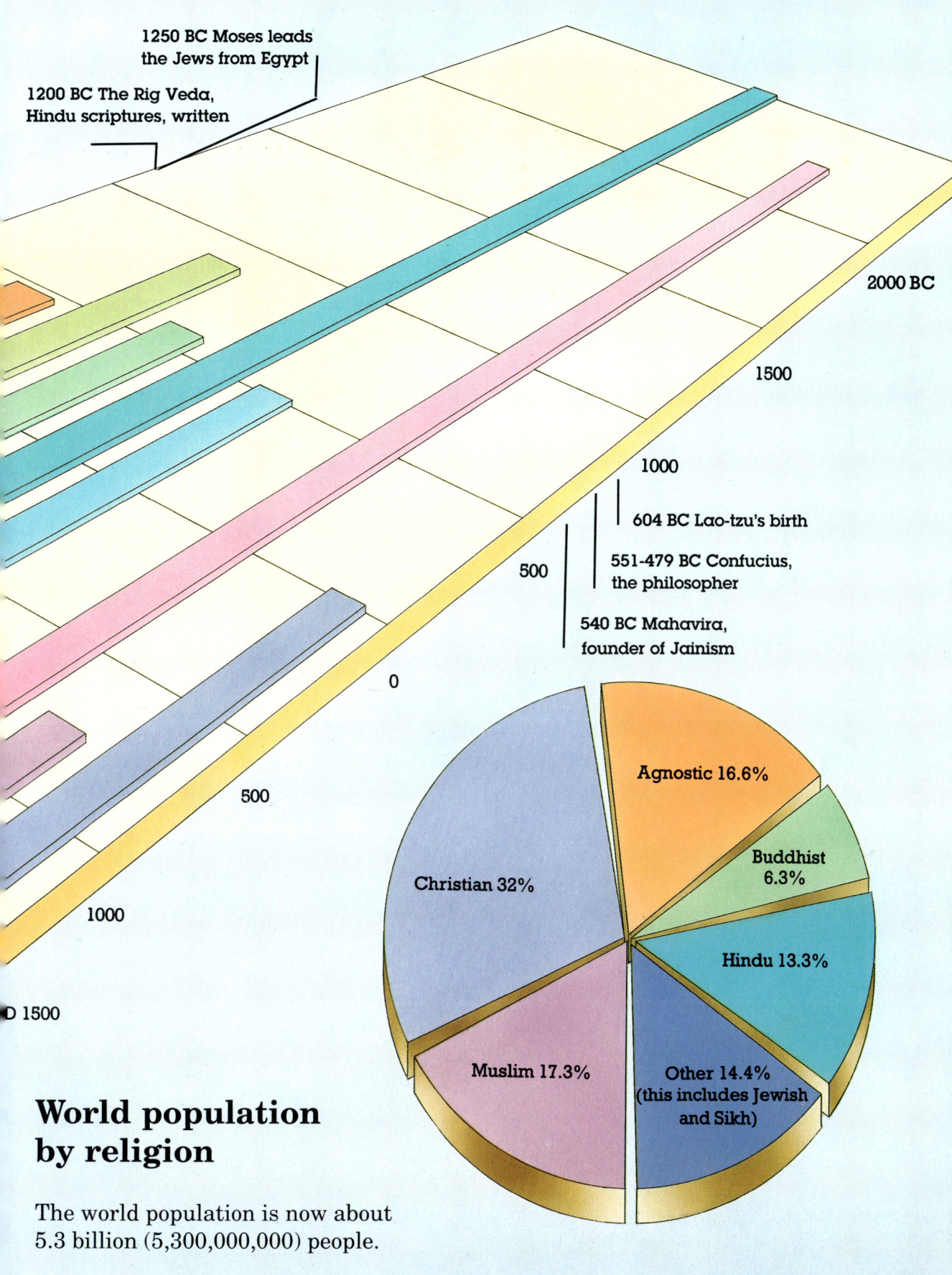

Glossary

Abraham: The man regarded as the founder of the Jewish faith. Christians and Muslims also think of him as a holy man.

Afterlife: The continued existence of someone's soul after the person's body dies.

Ahura Mazda: The name for the one God in the Parsee religion.

Anoint: To place oil on a person or an object as a sign of respect.

Bishop: A clergyman higher than a priest or minister. A bishop sometimes has special religious powers and duties.

Brahman: The highest divine force in Hinduism. Brahman is in all the gods and in everything that exists.

Caliphs: The rulers of Islam who came after the Prophet Muhammad.

Ceremony: A ritual act held to mark a special occasion, such as coming of age or marriage.

Confucius: Born in 551 BC, the founder of a philosophy of living based on respect and order.

Convert: To convince someone to change his or her beliefs, whether religious or otherwise.

Crusade: A holy war that Christians fought against Muslims in the Middle Ages.

Demon: An evil spirit or devil.

Dreamtime: The time, according to Australian Aboriginals, when supernatural beings created the world.

Druid: A priest or minister of religion among the ancient nations of Gaul, Britain, and Germany. Druids also knew some mathematics and natural science.

Eastern Orthodox church: A branch of the Christian church. It is widespread in eastern Europe, Greece, and Turkey.

Faith: A complete and total belief in something.

Fated: Decided ahead of time by some force. Some people believe that what happens in their lives is controlled by a guiding force.

Hare Krishna movement: A sect of Hinduism followed mainly by people in the West.

Holy Spirit: One of the three persons of God that Christians believe in. The other two are God, the Father, and Jesus, the Son.

Inquisition: A court set up by the Catholic church in the Middle Ages to try and punish people for not believing in Catholicism.

Karma: A word that explains that what happens in a person's present life results from what the person did in a past life. Karma is part of a belief in reincarnation.

Lao-tzu: The founder of the religion of Taoism. He also wrote the main book of Taoism in the first century BC.

Magic: An art that uses the force of spirits to do things that cannot be explained.

Meditation: Thinking deeply about some religious or spiritual thing.

Messiah: In Judaism, a man to be sent by God to restore the Jewish nation to its former power. Christians believe that Jesus Christ is the Messiah, who came to save people from sin.

Middle Ages: A period of European history from around AD 500 to 1500.

Migrate: To go from one place to settle in another.

Moses: The man who led the Jews from their captivity in Egypt to the Promised Land. He received the Ten Commandments from God.

Multicultural: Having many different cultures living together in one region or country.

Mummy: A body that has been preserved with salts and spices, then wrapped in linen cloths, so that it will not decay.

Mystical: A word describing things in a religion that are hard to explain, but must be believed.

Myth: A traditional story that tries to explain some natural happening or that tells the deeds of ancient gods and heroes.

Nanak: The founder of the Sikh religion. He lived from 1469 to 1539 and wrote many of the hymns that became part of the religion.

Parsee: A member of the ancient Zoroastrian religion of Persia (now Iran). Parsees fled from Muslim persecution in the ninth century AD and settled in India.

Persecute: To treat people badly because of their race or religion.

Philosophy: The beliefs and values that people live their lives by.

Pope: The head of the Roman Catholic church.

Puritans: Christian Protestants of the sixteenth and seventeenth centuries who wanted to "purify" the church of decoration and ceremony.

Queen of Sheba: A queen, of a country unknown today, who visited King Solomon in Israel. Legend says when she returned to her own country, she had converted to Judaism.

Reincarnation: The belief that those who die will be reborn into another body on Earth.

Roman Catholic church: One of the oldest branches of Christianity. The pope, the bishop of Rome, is its head.

Scriptures: The sacred writings of a religion. They usually contain the main teachings of the religion, and often rules for its followers.

Shakers: A Christian sect founded by Ann Lee in 1770. Shakers lead simple lives of work and service and do not marry. Men and women live separately in their communities.

Shrine: A holy place where people may come to worship privately.

Solstice: The time when the Sun is farthest from the equator. The summer solstice marks the longest day of the year. In the Northern Hemisphere, it usually falls on or near June 21. Some ancient religions marked this day with special ceremonies.

Soul: The part of a person that lives on after the body dies.

Spirit: A being without a body. A spirit is like a soul, but it may not ever have had a body.

Stonehenge: A circle made of huge stones in southern England, probably around 1500 BC. Some people believe it was once a druid temple.

Ten Commandments: The ten major laws that God gave to Moses. They form a key part of the Jewish and Christian religions.

Vishnu: One of the three main gods of the Hindu religion. He has ten different forms.

Wu wei: In Taoism, the way to follow in life. It means accepting what comes and not trying to change things.

Yahweh: The name of God in Judaism. At first it was spelled YHWH and was too sacred to say. In time it became Yahweh, and later Jehovah.

Index

A **boldface** number shows that the entry is illustrated on that page. The same page often has text about the entry, too.

Aboriginals 21
Abraham 34
Abu Bakr 49
afterlife, beliefs about 7, 14, **15**, 16-17, 26, 29, 33
agnosticism 57, **59**
Ahmadis (Muslim sect) 53
Ahura Mazda (Parsee God) 33
Allah (God) 48-49, 51, 52
Amaterasu (Japanese Sun goddess) 25
Amish (Christian sect) **47**
Analects (sayings of Confucius) 26
ancient religions **12-17**
Anglican church (see Church of England)
anointing 31
Aphrodite (Greek goddess) 16, **17**
apostles, Christian **40**, 41
Artemis (Greek goddess) 16, **17**
Aryans 28
Athena (Greek goddess) 16, **17**
Augustine, Saint 10
Augustus **17**
ayatollahs (Shi'ite Muslim leaders) **52**

Baha'i faith 55
bar mitzvah (Jewish coming-of-age ceremony) 36
beliefs 8-9
Bible **5**, 43
Book of the Dead **15**
Brahman (Hindu god) 29
Brahman (Hindu priest) 28
Buddha 22-**23**, 24, 58
Buddhism **5**, **22-25**, **58-59**

caliphs (Muslim leaders) 50, 52
Calvin, John (French theologian) **44**
caste system, Hindu 29, 32
cathedrals 7
chador (Muslim women's dress) **53**
chapels 7
Charon 17
"Children of God" 29
chi-rho (Christian symbol) **41**
Christ (see Jesus)
Christianity 9, 10, 36, **40-47**, 51, 56, **58-59**
    growth of **42-43**
    in the New World **46-47**
    origins of **40-41**
    and the Reformation **44-45**
    symbols of **5**, 41
Chuang Tzu (Taoist scriptures) 27
Church of England 45
churches 7, **56** (see also mosques, synagogues, *and* temples)
codes of life (as aspects of religion) 7
coming-of-age ceremonies
    Sikh 32
    Jewish 36
Confucianism **26-27**, **58-59**
Confucius **26**
Conservative Judaism **38**-39
convents 42
conversion, religious 10-11, 19
Cranmer, Thomas (archbishop of Canterbury) **45**
creation stories 6, 36
cremation 32
Crucifixion (of Jesus) 41
Crusades, the 51
cults, religious 55

dakhmas (Parsee towers of silence) **33**
Dashara (Hindu festival) 31
death ceremonies **32**, **33** (see also afterlife, beliefs about)
deities (see God, gods, *and* names of specific gods)
Diana (Roman goddess) 16, **17**
disciples, Jesus' **40**, 41
Diwali (Hindu festival) 31
Dreamtime, Aboriginal **21**
druids **12**
Durga (see Shakti)

Easter Island statues **19**
Eastern Orthodox church 43
Eden, Garden of 36
Egyptian religion, ancient 14-**15**
Eightfold Path, Noble 22, 23
Episcopal church (see Church of England)
Ethiopian Jews 38
evangelists 47
Exodus (of the Jews) 34-35

Far Eastern religions 8, 9, **22-27**
festivals (see names of specific festivals)
fish (as Christian symbol) 41
Five Pillars of Islam 52
Four Noble Truths 22, 23
Frank, Anne **35**
Frazer, Sir James **12**
Freya (Norse goddess) 13
fundamentalism 47

Galilee, Sea of **41**
Gandhi, Mahatma 29, **56**
Ganesh (Hindu god) **30**
Ganges River **28**
Gautama, Siddhartha (see Buddha)
Geldof, Bob **57**
God 6, 7, 8, 20, 29, 32, 34, 35, 36, 41, 45, 48, 49, 52, 54, 55 (see *also* Ahura Mazda, Allah, Jesus Christ, *and* Yahweh)
gods 4, 6, 7, 8, 15, 19, 33
    ancient 12-13
    Egyptian 14-**15**
    Greek and Roman **16-17**
    Hindu 8, 29, **30**-31
    (see also names of specific deities)
Gospels 43
Graham, Billy **47**
Great Mosque **48**
Greek religion, ancient **16-17**

Hades 16
hajj 52
Hare Krishna movement **54**, 55
Hasidic Judaism **38-39**
Hegira 50
Henry VIII (king of England) 45
Hera (Greek goddess) **16**
heresy (see Inquisition, Spanish)
Hermes (Greek god) 16, **17**
Hinduism **5**, **28-31**, 32, 56, **58-59**
    sadhu of **8**
    temple of **7**
holy orders (see monks)
Holy Spirit 41
holy wars, Muslim 50-51
Horus (Egyptian god) **15**
hsaio (Confucian principle) 26
Hutterites (Christian sect) 47

icons (sacred images) **42**
Inca religion 13
incarnations (see reincarnation)
India, religions of 24, **28-33**, 51
    Hinduism **5**, **28-31**, **32**, 56, **58-59**
    Jainism 33
    Parseeism 33
    Sikhism **32**, 58
Inquisition, Spanish 44, **45**

nuit mask **20**
lam **5**, 36, **48-53**, 56, **58-59**
   and mosques **6**, **48**, **50**
   and Muhammad 48-50
   sects of 52-53
   spread of **50-51**
rael 35

ainism **33**, **58-59**
apanese religion **9**, 24, 25
   (see also Buddhism
   and Shinto)
n (Confucian principle) 26
erusalem **35**, 51
esus 9, **40**-41, 58
ws (see Judaism)
had (holy war) 50-51
ns (Muslim genies) 51
odo and Jodo Shinsu (Buddhist
   sects) 25
daism **5**, **7**, 11, **34-39**, **58-59**
   beliefs of **34**-35, **36-37**, 40
   history of **34-35**
   movements of **38-39**
   spread of 35
das Iscariot 40
no (Roman goddess) **16**
piter (Roman god) **16**

ali (see Shakti)
rma 29
oran (Muslim scriptures) **5**, **49**,
   51, 52, 53
orean religion 24
sher food 37
rishna (see Hare Krishna
   movement and Vishnu)
ung Fu-tzu (see Confucius)

akshmi (Hindu goddess) 30
ao-tzu 27, 59
aw (Jewish) (see Torah)
aders 6-7, 10
   Hindu **8**
   Muslim 50, **52**-53
   Sikh 32
   (see also names of specific
   leaders)
e after death (see afterlife)
vingstone, David (missionary-
   explorer) 11
ther, Martin (German
   monk) **44**-45

agic 19
ahavira (founder of
   Jainism) 59
ahayana (Northern
   Buddhism) 24

Mary (mother of Jesus) **42**
mask, Inuit 20
Maya religion **13**
Mayflower (ship) **46-47**
Mecca **48**, 50
medical missionaries 11
meditation 6, 20, 23, 25, 29, 31
mediums, spirit **27**
Mennonites (Christian sect) 47
menorah (Jewish candle-
   stick) **37**
Mercury (Roman god) 16, **17**
Messiah, the 40
   Jesus as 40
   Ras Tafari as 55
Methodist church 47
minarets (see mosques)
Minerva (Roman goddess)
   16, **17**
ministers 6-7
missionaries **10**, 11, 19
mistletoe **13**
monasteries 42-**43**
monks
   Buddhist **22**
   Christian 42-**43**
Moon, Sun Myung 55
mortification of the flesh **29**
Moses **34**-35, 59
mosques (Islamic places of
   worship) **6**, **48**, **50**
Muhammad 48-49, 50, 52, 58
multiculturalism 56
mummies, Egyptian 14-**15**
Muslims (see Islam)
Myanmar, religion in 24
mystical religions 8-9, **10**-11

Nanak (founder of Sikhism)
   32, 58
nature, religion and 4, 18-19
Neptune (Roman god) **16**
New Testament (Christian
   scriptures) 43
Nichiren (Buddhist sect) 25
Nile River **14**
Noble Eightfold Path 22, **23**
Noble Truths, Four 22, **23**
nomads, African **18**
Norse gods **13**
North American Indian religions
   20-21
nuns **42**

Old Testament (Christian
   scriptures) 43
Olympus, Mount 16
Orthodox Judaism 38, **39**
   Hasidic sect of **38-39**

Osiris (Egyptian god) 14, **15**

Parseeism **33**
Passover (Jewish festival) 34
persecution
   of Christians 42
   of Jews **11** , 35
philosophy and religion 26, 27
pilgrimages **48**
Pilgrims **46-47**
places of worship 6 (see also
   churches, mosques,
   synagogues, and temples)
pope 42, **43**, 45
Poseidon (Greek god) **16**
prayer 6
   Muslim **49**
preachers 47
priests 6-7
   druid **12**
   Egyptian 14
   Hindu **28**
   Shinto women **9**
Promised Land 34, 35
Prophet, the (see Muhammad)
prophetic religions 8, 9
prophets and prophecies 8, 9,
   37, 40
proselytism (see conversion,
   religious and missionaries)
Protestantism **44-45**, **46**-47
purifying the soul **29**
Puritans **46-47**

rabbis (Jewish religious leaders)
   7, **36**, 37
Rama (see Vishnu)
Ramadan (Muslim month and
   observance) 49, 52
Rastafarianism **54**, 55
Reform Judaism 38-39
Reformation, Protestant **44-45**
reincarnation 7, 22, 29, 32, 33
Resurrection (of Jesus) 41
Rig Veda (Hindu scriptures) 59
rock carvings **21**
Roman Catholicism **42-43**, 44, **45**
Roman religion, ancient **16-17**

Sabbath, Jewish 37
sacred writings (see scriptures)
sadhu (Hindu holy man) **8**
salat 52
sawm 52
scriptures **5**, 6, 7
   Buddhist **23**
   Christian **5**, 43
   Confucian 26
   Egyptian 14, **15**

Hindu **28-29**, 59
Jewish 36-37, 40
Muslim **5**, **49**, 51, 52, 53
Taoist 27
(*see also* names of specific scriptures)
shahada 52
Shakti (Hindu goddess) 31
Sheba, queen of 38
Shi'ites (Muslim sect) **52-53**
Shingon (Buddhist sect) 25
Shintoism **9**, 25, **58-59**
Shiva (Hindu god) 30
shrines 13, **25**, 31
Sikhism **5**, **32**, **58-59**
skullcap, Jewish **37**
Spain, Muslim influences in **50**, **51**
spirit medium, Taoist **27**
spirits 25
Styx, River 16
Sumerian religion 15
Sun worship 4, 12, 25
Sunnites (Muslim sect) 52
symbols, religious **5**, **25**, **41**
synagogues (Jewish places of worship) 7, **36**, 37

tallith (Jewish prayer shawl) **37**
Tanakh (Jewish scriptures) 36-37, 38
Tao Te Ching (Taoist scriptures) 27
Taoism **27**, **58-59**
temples **6**, **7**, 13, 16
    Buddhist **6**, 23
    Confucian **26**
    Hindu **7**, **30**
Ten Commandments 35
Tendai (Buddhist sect) 25
Teresa, Mother **57**
Thailand, religion in 24
Theravada (Southern Buddhism) 24
Thor (Norse god) 13
Tibetan religion 24, **25**
tombs 14
Torah 36, 37
totem poles **20**
towers of silence (*see dakhmas*)
tribal religions **18-21**
Trinity, Christian 41
Tripitaka (Buddhist scriptures) **23**
Truths, Four Noble 22, 23

Unification church **55**
Untouchables (Hindu caste) 29

Vatican City 43

Venus (Roman goddess) 16, **17**
Vishnu (Hindu god) 8, **30**

Wailing Wall (*see* Western Wall)
Wesley, John **46**, 47
Western Wall **35**
Woden (Norse god) 13
wu wei (Taoist belief) 27

Yahweh (Jewish God) 34
    (*see also* God)
yarmulke (Jewish skullcap) **37**
Yellow Hats (Buddhist sect) **25**
Yuletide (origin of term) 13

zakat 52
Zen Buddhism **24**, 25
Zeus (Greek god) 16

Hilltop Elem. Library
West Unity, OH